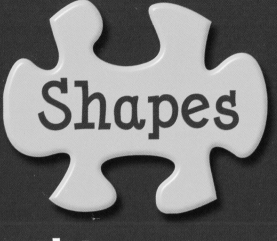

Shapes

Stars

by Sarah L. Schuette

Reading Consultant:

Elena Bodrova, Ph.D., Senior Consultant

Mid-continent Research for Education and Learning

an imprint of Capstone Press

Mankato, Minnesota

A+ Books are published by Capstone Press
P.O. Box 669, 151 Good Counsel Drive, Mankato, Minnesota 56002
http://www.capstone-press.com

1 2 3 4 5 6 07 06 05 04 03 02

Library of Congress Cataloging-in-Publication Data
Schuette, Sarah L., 1976–
    Stars / by Sarah L. Schuette.
    p.cm—(Shapes)
    Summary: Simple text, photographs, and illustrations show star shapes in everyday objects.
    Includes bibliographical references and index.
    ISBN 0-7368-1464-7 (hardcover)
    I. Stars (Shape)—Juvenile literature. [1.Stars (Shape)] Title.
QA482 .S383 2003
516'.15—dc21   2002000897

Created by the A+ Team

Sarah L. Schuette, editor; Heather Kindseth, art director and designer; Jason Knudson, designer
    and illustrator; Angi Gahler, illustrator; Gary Sundermeyer, photographer; Nancy White,
    photographer and photo stylist

Note to Parents, Teachers, and Librarians
The Shapes series uses color photographs and a nonfiction format to introduce children to the shapes around them. It is designed to be read aloud to a pre-reader or to be read independently by an early reader. The images help early readers and listeners understand the text and concepts discussed. The book encourages further learning by including the following sections: Table of Contents, Words to Know, Read More, Internet Sites, and Index. Early readers may need assistance using these features.

Table of Contents

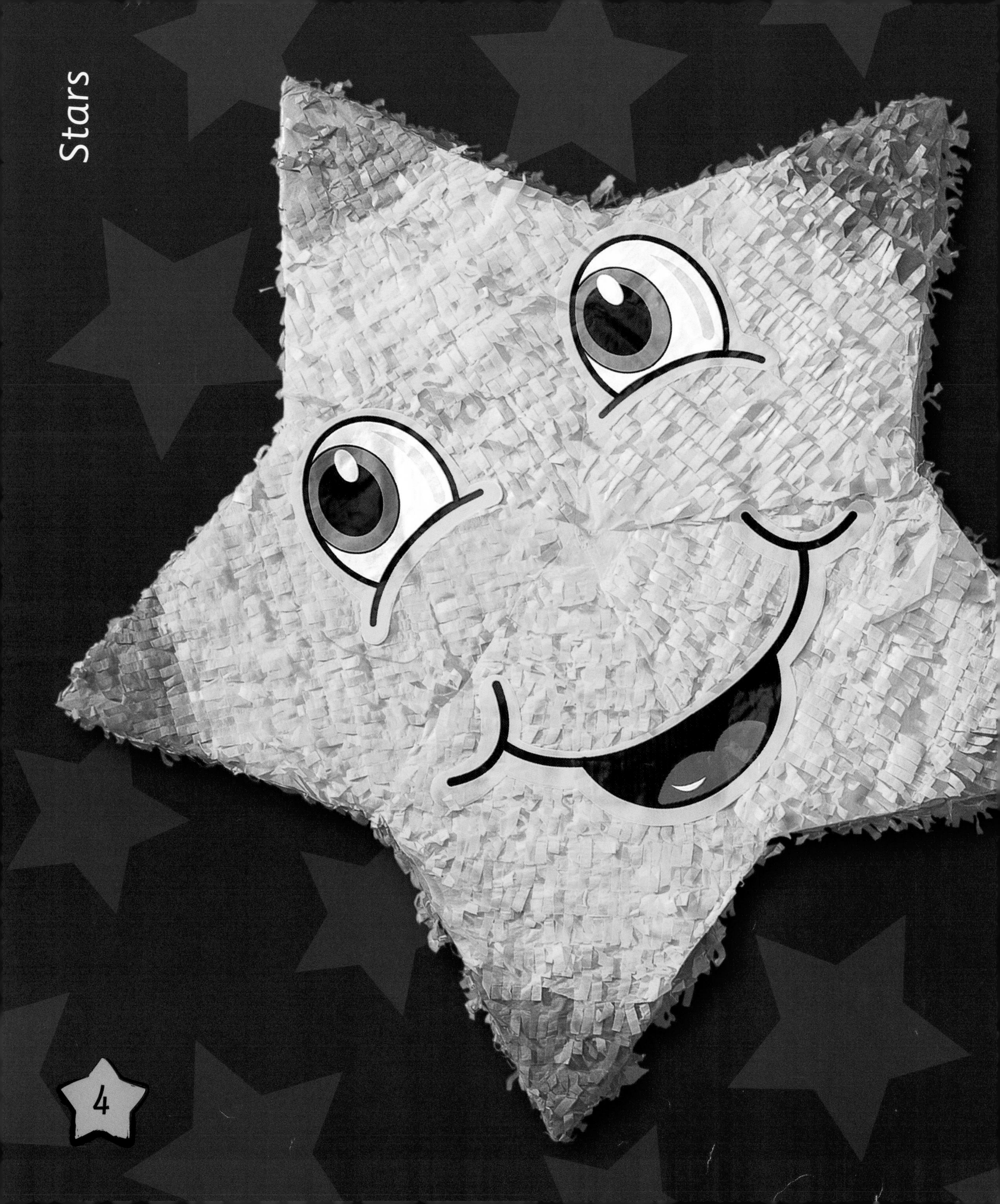

Stars are shapes
pointy and bright.

Stars give off a
glowing light.

6

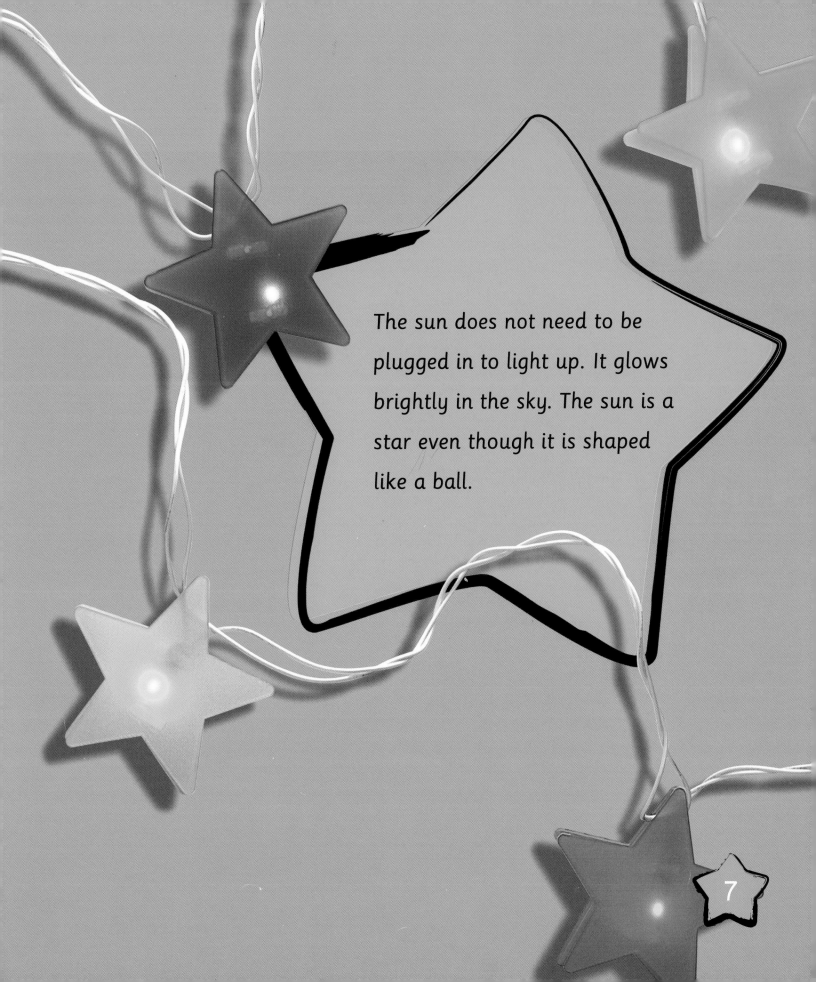

The sun does not need to be plugged in to light up. It glows brightly in the sky. The sun is a star even though it is shaped like a ball.

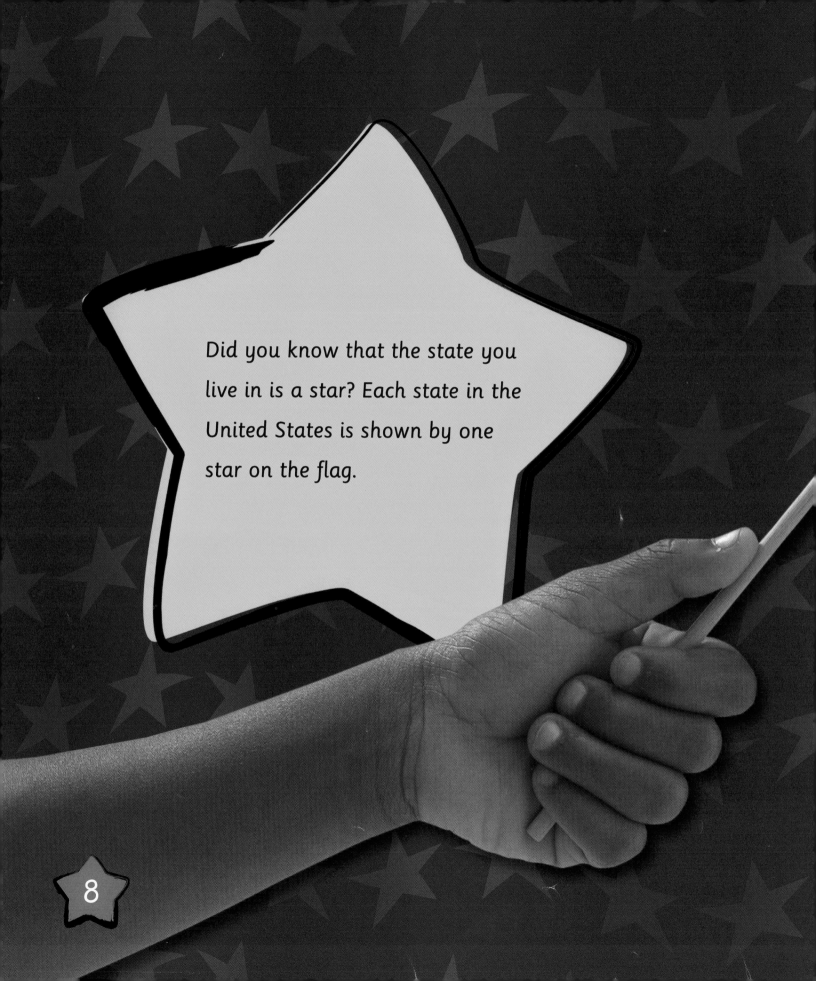

Did you know that the state you live in is a star? Each state in the United States is shown by one star on the flag.

Stars stand for
states on a flag.

9

Wrap up a gift in this star bag.

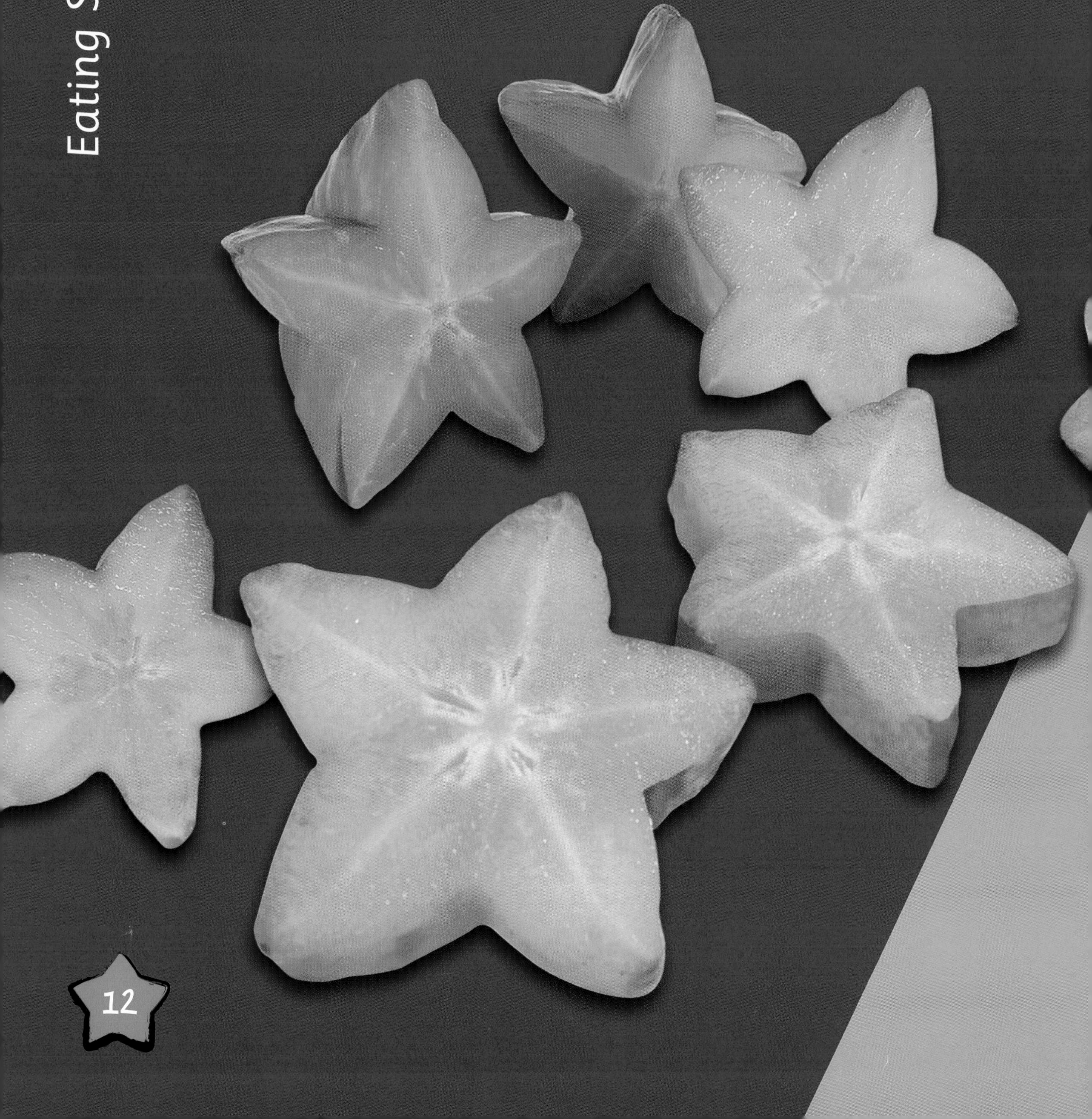

Star fruits have pointy edges on the outside. Slices of the fruit are shaped like stars.

Star fruit slices taste so sweet.

13

Cookies are stars
you like to eat.

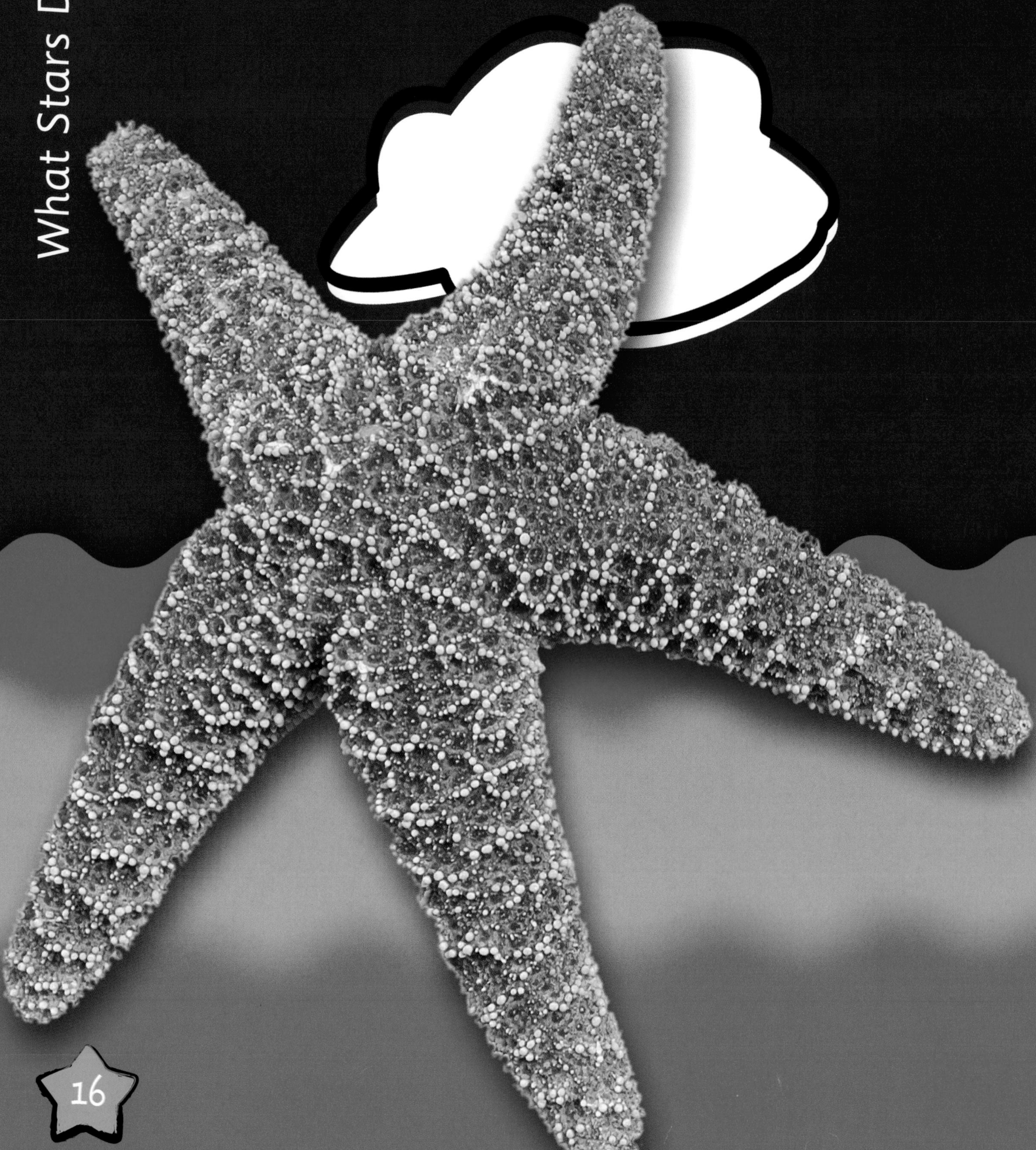

Wow! If a sea star loses an arm, it can grow back.

Sea stars live in the salty ocean.

17

Star wands wave in
a zigzag motion.

18

Look outside at night. The stars you see are giant balls of burning gases. There are millions of stars that glow in the night sky.

Stars glow after you go to bed.

22

Star hats sit on top of your head.

Math Test

$$3 + 2 = 5$$

$$5 - 3 = 2$$

$$1 + 5 = 6$$

Gold stars mean
a perfect test.

Find the star that is stuck on this vest.

27

Make Star Magnets

You will need

different colors of clay
or modeling material
star cookie cutters
self-adhesive magnets

1 Flatten the clay or modeling material with your hand.

2 Press the cookie cutters down on the clay. Let your stars sit overnight to dry.

3 Attach the magnets to the back of the stars.

29

Words to Know

flag—a piece of cloth with a pattern on it; a flag is a symbol of a country; the flag of the United States is called the Stars and Stripes.

glow—to give off a steady light

ocean—the large body of saltwater that covers most of the earth's surface; many animals and plants live in the ocean.

sea star—an ocean animal with five or more arms; a sea star is sometimes called a starfish because it is shaped like a star.

star fruit—a fruit that grows in warm places; a piece of star fruit tastes a little like a pear.

zigzag—a movement with short, sharp turns from one side to the other

30

Read More

Burke, Jennifer S. *Stars.* City Shapes. New York: Children's Press, 2000.

Patilla, Peter. *Starting off with Shapes.* Hauppauge, New York: Barron's, 2001.

Rau, Dana Meachen. *A Star in My Orange: Looking for Nature's Shapes.* Brookfield, Conn.: Millbrook Press, 2002.

Salzmann, Mary Elizabeth. *Stars.* What Shape Is It? Edina, Minn.: Abdo, 2000.

Internet Sites

Track down many sites about star shapes.
Visit the FACT HOUND at *http://www.facthound.com*

IT IS EASY! IT IS FUN!

1) Go to *http://www.facthound.com*
2) Type in: 0736814647
3) Click on "FETCH IT" and FACT HOUND will find several links hand-picked by our editors.

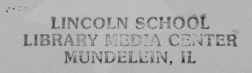

Relax and let our pal FACT HOUND do the research for you!

Index